Original title:
Life's Meaning: It's Complicated

Copyright © 2025 Creative Arts Management OÜ
All rights reserved.

Author: Levi Montgomery
ISBN HARDBACK: 978-1-80566-133-7
ISBN PAPERBACK: 978-1-80566-428-4

The Intersection of Fate and Chance

Two paths forked by a squirrel's gaze,
I flipped a coin in a dreamy haze.
One side's the river, the other's a climb,
I chose the wrong route, oh, every time!

A chicken crossed, just to stake her claim,
While I was pondering, who's to blame?
Fate's a joker, with a laugh track loud,
Chance is the jester, always in the crowd.

Whirlwinds of Thought in Stillness.

In silence, thoughts dance like bees in flight,
Buzzing around, oh what a delight!
They hit a wall, then swirl and spin,
Stillness is chaos, where do I begin?

A riddle wrapped in a funny hat,
I search for answers in the kitchen cat.
The fridge hums loud, like a stand-up show,
Finding humor in places where wisdom won't go.

The Tangle of Existence

Twisted vines of reason and rhyme,
I tried to untangle them over time.
Hiding from logic while seeking some fun,
Lost in the labyrinth, where's the exit run?

A noodle of fate and a spaghetti strand,
Twisted together, they misunderstood the plan.
With every fork, the pasta does twist,
In a bowl of confusion, I'm lost in the mist.

Whispers in the Fog

Fog speaks softly, a whisper at dawn,
Promises made, yet quickly they're gone.
A ghost of a thought, it giggles away,
As I chase the shadows of the things they say.

In the grayness, I trip on my own two feet,
Trying to dance with ghosts, isn't it sweet?
The meaning's eluding, it's hard to see clear,
But at least I can laugh at my own silly fear.

Unpacking the Unknown

In boxes piled high, I search for the truth,
A sock and a sandwich, but where's all the poof?

The map to my purpose is lost on the way,
With GPS broken, I'm stuck in dismay.

I ask my goldfish for thoughts on the quest,
He bubbles profound, but he's chasing his jest.

With each twist and turn, I trip on my shoe,
Perhaps it's the journey that matters, who knew?

The Web of Intertwined Lives

We're tangled like spaghettis, all sauces and glee,
A friend borrowed money, now owes it to me.

In coffee shops gossiping, tales intertwine,
A cat and a dog share a dream that seems fine.

In the chaos, we flourish, like weeds in the sun,
Though figuring out why, can feel like a run.

With laughter and feuds, we dance on the thread,
Life's a grand circus, just hold on your head!

The Timing of Tomorrow

The clock strikes too soon, or so it would seem,
   I'm late to the party, or lost in a dream.

Tomorrow's a riddle, a puzzle to crack,
But right now, I'm focused on snacks and a nap.

The universe chuckles at plans that I make,
  My calendar laughs as it bends, gives a shake.

Though moments slip by like jelly on toast,
  I'll savor the fun, that's what matters most!

A Tangle of Hopes and Fears

In a garden where dreams sprout,
Hopes twist like spaghetti, no doubt.
Fears dance in circles, so sly,
Eating ice cream as tears pass by.

Life wears a hat, quite askew,
Juggling lemons, while sipping brew.
Optimism high, like a kite,
Winds of doubt give it a fright.

When Questions Become Characters

They stroll the streets with quizzical grins,
'What's the point?' asks a man with fins.
'Why move fast?' whines a turtle slow,
Drawing crowds with its awkward show.

Each question wears a funny hat,
Contemplating where the bananas are at.
Debates turn into slapstick fights,
As laughter echoes through starry nights.

The Enigma of Silent Choices

Two paths diverge in a quirky park,
One's lit with sparkles, the other, dark.
Do you choose the ice cream stand?
Or wander off to the magic band?

Choices whisper in a cryptic tone,
Like socks that vanish, leaving you alone.
A dance of options in silly flares,
While ducks quack truths that no one dares.

Of Mountains and Molehills

I climbed a hill, thought it was grand,
But tripped on a rock, now I'm buried in sand.
Mountains loom, so high and wide,
While molehills tease from the other side.

Chasing peaks with a wild, goofy grin,
Only to find it's a game I can't win.
With laughter echoing throughout the day,
I smile and say, 'Let's dance anyway!'

Tides of Thought

In the sea of dreams we float,
Waves of worry, a silly boat.
Some thoughts sink like stones all day,
While others dance and drift away.

Juggling choices, we often trip,
Like clowns on a wobbly ship.
Is that a wave or a weird fish?
We laugh and hope for a nice swish!

Life's a puzzle, missing pieces,
But who needs sense when humor increases?
Sailing through chaos can be sweet,
With laughter as our life's retreat.

The Color of Uncertainty

Gray skies whisper, 'What's next? Find out!'
Colors clash with a joyful shout.
Red for the love, blue for the blues,
Mix them up and you'll find clues.

We paint our days with strokes of chance,
With every twist, a quirky dance.
Is it orange, pink, or just plain green?
Each hue holds secrets, unforeseen!

But amidst the swirl, we can't forget,
The bright side's shining, no need to fret.
Life's a canvas, a colorful spree,
Painted with laughter, just let it be!

Footprints in the Sand

On the shore, we leave our mark,
Wiggly lines, not a single arc.
Every step a goofy twist,
Did I forget something? Oh, I must insist!

The tide rolls in with a playful splash,
Washing away my fumbles and trash.
Every footprint tells a tale,
Of mishaps, giggles, and an occasional wail.

Finding direction from sand's embrace,
Is much like venturing into space.
Floating in dreams, what could be grand?
Oh look, more footprints, all out of hand!

The Choir of Choices

A symphony of options sings,
With funny notes and silly flings.
Do I choose this? Or take that path?
Life's a concert with a giggle and a laugh.

Each choice a note in a crazy tune,
Dancing under a dappled moon.
One step forward, a hop to the side,
Join the chorus, let spontaneity be your guide.

Alto, tenor, who knows the score?
Maybe I'll play on the kitchen floor.
Life's a melody shared with a friend,
And giggles echo until the end!

The Intersection of Self

In a world full of memes,
I ponder my schemes,
Am I here for the cake,
Or just for the dreams?

Mirror, mirror, on the wall,
Does your feedback stall?
Or maybe you just reflect,
A questionable ball?

As I juggle my quirks,
With my muddled perks,
I map out my thoughts,
And create my own works.

A selfie with a twist,
On my 'to-do' list,
Finding meaning in snacks,
Is a life without risk?

Shadows of Dreams

Chasing shadows that tease,
On a whim, with such ease,
I trip over my wishes,
Just trying to appease.

Dreams whisper my name,
In a wild, silly game,
Yet I stumble around,
And forget why I came.

With my head in the clouds,
And my heart in the crowds,
I laugh at my chaos,
In life's staring shrouds.

Though my path may be bent,
And my thoughts often spent,
I'll dance through confusion,
With a jokester's intent.

The Lace of Longing

In a closet of wishes,
Where hope rarely swishes,
I search through the lace,
For the quirks and the swishes.

Longing ties me down,
In a whimsical gown,
Twists and turns guide my feet,
In this circus of clowns.

With dreams entangled tight,
And laughter at night,
I tie strings of desire,
And hope all feels right.

As I weave through this thread,
With a giggle, I tread,
Finding joy in the mess,
Though the needle is red.

Broken Compass

My compass is on strike,
It won't budge, not a like,
Should I follow the stars,
Or just hike with a bike?

Lost in a world of choice,
I listen to my inner voice,
It says, 'Get a hot fudge,'
And just rejoice!

The direction is a joke,
Like my last piece of smoke,
Navigating nonsense,
Till I find a good bloke.

With a grin on my face,
I wander through space,
A broken compass? Maybe,
But I'm still in the race!

Found Direction

Turns out, it's a circle,
With some laughs and some wrinkles,
I found my way back,
In a tangle of sprinkles.

Through the maze of my thoughts,
In a land full of knots,
I discovered the truth,
With some giggles and shots.

My direction is a dance,
With a clumsy romance,
Every step feels foolish,
Yet I take every chance.

With my heart set on fun,
And a quirky pun,
I twirl through the chaos,
Till the day is done.

A Riddle of Clouds

Fluffy pillows drift up high,
Wonder how they float, oh my!
Do they gossip, share a joke?
Or are they just a vapor cloak?

Raindrops fall with a sassy splash,
Is it joy, or just a crash?
Thunder claps, like laughter loud,
A cosmic punchline in a cloud.

Sunrise paints a coffee scene,
With colors bright, and in between,
A sip of light, a wink of day,
Oh, the games the heavens play!

So up above, they keep it light,
Creating quirks to our delight.
Clouds may be wise, though coy and vague,
In their riddle, the world's a stage.

Beneath the Surface

Bubbles rise in playful cheer,
What's below is far from clear.
Fish in suits swim past with speed,
Talking business, planting seed.

Coral reefs are nature's show,
Dressed to impress, they steal the glow.
Crabs do salsa on the sand,
In a dance that's simply grand.

Secrets lurk where light won't dare,
Some say treasure, some despair.
Yet the giggles of the tide,
Make us wonder, what's the ride?

In a swirl of ocean's fun,
Life's a joke beneath the sun.
Sink or swim, take a chance,
Underwater, life's a dance!

Threads in the Tapestry

Colors woven, oh so bright,
Each thread whispers, takes a flight.
Some go straight, others might twirl,
In a fabric swirl, we unfurl.

A stitch of chaos, a dash of grace,
Patterns change in this wild space.
Knots of laughter, tears of woe,
All together, they steal the show.

Grandma's quilt holds tales untold,
Of days gone by, both young and old.
Each square a puzzle, piece of jest,
Life's a quilt—who knew it'd be a test?

In every twist, a chuckle hides,
Life's adventures, where joy abides.
Stitch by stitch, we weave our plan,
In this wacky world, we all can!

The Dance of Shadows

Underneath the bright moon's glance,
Shadows take the floor to dance.
Darkness winks with every sway,
Laughing softly, come what may.

Figures twist in ghostly play,
Making jokes in their ballet.
Flickering lights, a fitting tune,
These shadowy friends make the night a boon.

Costumed misfits, what a sight!
In their masquerade so light.
Bouncing off the walls with ease,
They trip and giggle in the breeze.

So let us join the nightly jest,
In laughter's arms, we're truly blessed.
For shadows know the best routines,
In every twist, a punchline gleans.

Hues of the Heart

Colors swirl in every heart,
Red for love, green for tart.
Yellow laughs, and blue does cry,
Orange dreams of pie up high.

Mix them all in one big bowl,
Stir the chaos, lose control.
Throw in giggles, sprinkle glee,
Who knew hearts could be so free?

Seasons of the Soul

Spring brings sprouts of joy so bright,
Summer's sun feels just so right.
Autumn leaves dance with a grin,
Winter snows hide all within.

Each season spins a funny tale,
Like socks that vanish in the pale.
Embrace the chills and sunbeams too,
For each has quirks, just like you!

The Balance Between Chaos and Order

A tightrope walker on a string,
One wrong step, it's quite the fling!
With juggling balls of daily tasks,
Life's a circus, wear those masks!

Order smiles with proper plans,
While chaos sneezes, spills, and jams.
Find the spark in every blunder,
Laughter's there—just look for thunder!

Cracks in the Facade

Oh, look at me, I'm put together,
But watch out now—stormy weather!
Behind my smile, a secret's spun,
Naps and snacks, oh what fun!

Chips and dips in my grand charade,
A little mess, yet unafraid.
Life's backyard looks quite absurd,
But in the chaos, joy's assured!

Fragments of Eternity

In a world of mixed signals, I tread,
Chasing my thoughts while eating bread.
They say it's deep, a puzzle you see,
But I can't find the pieces near my tea.

Juggling dreams while balancing bills,
Hoping to catch a rush from the thrills.
What feels profound often slips like soap,
In a bathtub of questions, my only hope.

Philosophers ponder while I just grin,
Do I need wisdom, or just a spin?
The universe winks, oh how it teases,
As I juggle my socks, and fend off sneezes.

So here I stand, a jester in thought,
With a crown of confusion, and a gift I brought.
Not the answers, but laughs to share,
On this wild trip, take the silly dare!

Echoes of the Unseen

I tap dance on dreams, dressed as a clown,
Searching for meaning while wearing a frown.
The whispers of wisdom float in the air,
Yet I'm lost in a maze without a care.

What's the purpose, oh silly old quest?<nSocks in the dryer, they vanish — a jest!
Each mystery looms like a cat with a grin,
Pawing at questions, I can't even begin.

With ticklish thoughts and a noodle-like mind,
I follow the echoes, with fun I'm entwined.
For every deep question, there's laughter to find,
As I juggle my quirks, the absurdity's kind.

So let's toast to the riddles, the giggles, the fun,
Life's a circus, not a race to be run.
With echoes of nonsense and quirks that abound,
Together we spin, dizzy, light-hearted, unbound!

The Labyrinth of Being

In this maze of existence, I twirl and I spin,
Searching for answers while clad in a grin.
The walls are adorned with the memes of the wise,
But I just get lost in a sea of goodbyes.

Round corners I wander, with snacks in my bag,
Attempting to grasp the elusive old wag.
Oh, the riddles they throw like confetti in air,
Yet I chuckle instead, with no burden to bear.

Each twist is a riddle, each turn a new dance,
Plenary paradox: I'll take my chance!
With humor as compass, my life's merry song,
The best part of wandering? You can't be wrong!

So pass me the cookie while lifting a cheer,
Laughing at chaos, I've nothing to fear.
In this labyrinth of being, let irony reign,
For in foolish delight, we all share the gain!

Unraveling the Enigma

An enigma, they say, full of twists and glee,
Yet I can't help wondering, what's there to see?
With a side of irony, I hunt for the clue,
My coffee cup spills; oh, what joy to pursue!

Some ponder and ponder, but I just sit still,
Snacking on questions with a laughter-filled thrill.
What's true and what's false? It's all mixed up right,
Perhaps being goofy is the ultimate sight.

Oh, the riddles they sing in a chorus so bright,
Like socks that go missing in the wash every night.
With absurdity as armor and smiles as my shield,
I embrace all the chaos this universe yields.

So here I unravel, with chuckles and quips,
Twirling on life's rollercoaster, enjoying the trips.
In this dance of the curious, we sway hand in hand,
Finding meaning in nonsense, it's perfectly grand!

The Quest for Belonging

In a world of quirks and highs,
We chase connection, oh my,
With mismatched socks and silly hats,
Searching for friends who share our chats.

In puppy parks and cafes bright,
We stumble, giggle, take flight,
As awkward hugs and laughter grow,
In the maze of 'who's that?' we flow.

Lost in thoughts, we often stray,
But find our way in a quirky way,
Like socks that never find a pair,
We're complete with love and care.

So here's to the odd and the strange,
In this colorful life we range,
For belonging isn't black or white,
It's painted in shades of laugh and light.

A Patchwork of Voices

Listen close, you'll hear the mix,
Of things we say and all our fix,
A patchwork quilt of shouts and glee,
As we argue who makes the best tea.

With jokes that tumble, twist, and fly,
Like popcorn kernels in the sky,
We weave our stories, loud and bright,
Making sense in the weird twilight.

Each voice a thread in a vibrant scheme,
Stitched together like some weird dream,
From who forgot the last bit of cake,
To laughs that make our sides shake.

So let's embrace the talk and cheer,
For every voice is welcome here,
In this chatter we delight and spin,
Where every goof is sure to win.

Moments Between Breath

Caught in the spaces, we sometimes freeze,
While pondering life's quirks with such ease,
In funny pauses, we take a flight,
Like a sneeze held back just feels right.

Amid the rush of daily grind,
We laugh at the weirdness we find,
Like when the toast lands butter-side down,
Or wearing mismatched shoes in town.

In these moments, we twirl and spin,
Chasing that sparkle beneath our skin,
The funny antics we guys deploy,
Are threads that weave together joy.

So let's breathe deep in this comical dance,
And seize the seconds with silly chance,
For inside the chaos and little mess,
We find the joy, we must confess.

The Silent Conversations

In crowded rooms, we share the air,
With silent glances, a secret dare,
A raised eyebrow, a wink or two,
Like we're all in on something new.

With smiles that bloom like crazy flowers,
We exchange our thoughts in just a hour,
Navigating jokes with a dance of grace,
Like a mime on a bustling space.

In shadows, whispers come to play,
As laughter bounces in a wobbly way,
We bond in silence, so absurd,
With memes and gestures yet unheard.

So here's to those quiet, laughing nights,
Where unspoken words take glorious flights,
For in the silence, we truly bind,
With fun and quirks combined, we find.

Tattered Maps of Memory

Old maps lead to treasure, but where's the gold?
X marks the spot, or so I've been told.
Lost in the forest, I stumble and trip,
Just following breadcrumbs, not taking a sip.

The compass spins wildly, it's lost its way,
Is north where I'm going, or did it decay?
Every path has a story, a laugh or a scream,
Navigating life's puzzles, a topsy-turvy dream.

With each twist and turn, I can't help but grin,
The confusion is charming—let the weirdness begin.
A map drawn in crayon, with glitter and flair,
In the chaos of moments, there's magic to share.

So let's hug the hiccups, embrace every mess,
In this grand adventure, we'll never digress.
Tattered maps reveal what we cannot see,
With laughter as our guide, we'll just let it be.

The Serendipity of Serpents

Serpents in suits, they waltz in a line,
Wiggling through situations, making me pine.
With each paradoxical twist, I cackle hard,
When life serves up snakes, it's like playing cards.

I trip over wisdom, slip on its tail,
It whispers sweet nothings, begins to unveil.
Each fumble a fortune, each tumble a score,
Unexpected confetti at every closed door.

They say fate has a smile, dressed up in a grin,
But who knew it slithers, with a daring kin?
In gardens of chaos where contradictions bloom,
I laugh at the serpents, they dance with the doom.

So let's twirl and tangle, let life throw the dice,
Embrace all the quirks, they are far more than nice.
For in this wild waltz with the snakes all around,
We find joy in the journey, where laughter is found.

Rimmed with Possibility

Around the edges, where dreams like to play,
Possibility beckons, "Come out for the day!"
With a wiggle and giggle, I tiptoe along,
Sipping on sunshine, humming a song.

What if I turn left? Or hop on one foot?
Each choice is a dance, in a bright, silly suit.
Like juggling with jellybeans, sweeter than pie,
Let's craft our adventures, and give them a try.

The rim of the glass, it's half-full, you see,
With splashes of whimsy, just waiting for tea.
Lemons and sugar make quite the delight,
In the chaos of choices, we'll dance through the night.

So here's to the moments, the maybes and "uh-ohs,"
Embrace every detour, wherever it goes.
Rimmed with the glimmer of things yet to come,
Let's toast to the laughter that's already begun.

The Orchestra of Silent Moments

A symphony plays in the pauses we keep,
With silence as music, so soothing, so deep.
Notes flutter like butterflies, dancing with glee,
In the quietest corners, is where we are free.

The triangle tinkles, the violins sigh,
As whispers flutter like sparks in the sky.
With the conductor bemused, in a topsy-turvy tune,
An unexpected harmony, crafted by noon.

In awkward soliloquies, the punchlines arrive,
With laughter and chaos, we truly survive.
Each silence a heartbeat, a wink or a glance,
In the orchestra of moments, we twirl and we prance.

So grab a few giggles, and share them around,
In the rhythm of life, let joy be unbound.
For even in quiet, where secrets reside,
There's a vibrant crescendo in every wild ride.

A Whisper in the Wind

A squirrel whispered, 'What's my goal?'
Yet climbed the tree to steal a roll.
He danced on branches, a jester bold,
While nuts spilled down like tales retold.

The breeze just laughed, a cheeky tease,
Said, 'Not all wisdom comes with ease!'
The acorn dreams of being grand,
Yet rests alone in this vast land.

One day a kite, so high it soared,
Tangled in branches, it couldn't hoard.
The squirrel chuckled, 'Oh what a plight!'
Yet down it came, in pure delight.

So as we chase each wish we crave,
Remember the antics, be bold but brave.
For life's a jest, with laughter's grin,
A whisper found, where dreams begin.

Charting the Uncharted

With a map upside down, I sailed the seas,
Hoping for treasures, not just a tease.
The compass spun, just like my brain,
I laughed aloud, 'This is insane!'

An octopus grinned, as I lost my way,
Waved eight arms, like it knew the play.
I asked for directions with a goofy smile,
It inked a pothole, 'You'll be here a while!'

The gulls they squawked in fitting glee,
Plotting my course, while sipping tea.
Each wave a giggle, each storm a jest,
Who knew the journey could be such a fest?

So here I am, with laughter in tow,
Charting my way where the silly winds blow.
The unknown beckons with a playful wink,
Navigating joy, not stopping to think.

The Canvas of Experience

With paintbrush in hand, I splattered away,
Colors of chaos on a sunny day.
A canvas of life in every hue,
Split with coffee stains and a shoe too.

My cat jumped in, thinking it grand,
Paw prints of wisdom, a master plan.
A rainbow beast, with fur of delight,
Laughing at me, in the morning light.

Each stroke a tale, both wacky and wild,
Yet here I am, a confused child.
Life's palette mixed with doubt and cheer,
An artful mess, but I hold it dear.

So join me now, in this whirly whirl,
As we dance in colors, give fate a twirl.
For in this canvas, both thick and thin,
The joy of creating, where laughs begin.

Navigating the Abyss

In depths so deep, where shadows play,
I fell in a puddle, found hope today.
With laughter bubbles rising high,
I splashed around, 'Oh me, oh my!'

An eel sang songs of love and pain,
His voice was flat, like a runaway train.
I wobbled closer, hand on my chin,
'Is this a concert, or a swim to win?'

Around me swirled both fish and fate,
Holding a banquet of things they hate.
Yet in their grumbling, a chorus emerged,
Sing loud, swim proud, where dreams are surged.

So deeper I go, in my silly quest,
Navigating the chaos, a quirky jest.
For in the abyss, I find my spark,
A giggle afloat in the deepening dark.

The Fill of Void

In a world where socks just vanish,
We search for them in every niche,
Hoping to find that long-lost pair,
While wearing sandals, feeling rich.

Bananas speaking to each other,
With wisdom wrapped in their peel,
If only we could take advice,
From fruits that know just how to feel.

Chasing dreams that like to hide,
They giggle and dart away so fast,
Like that one friend who always leaves,
Before dessert, when the fun is vast.

Here's to questions with no answers,
To mysteries that tickle the brain,
Like trying to explain the humor,
In puns that are really quite plain.

Portraits of Introspection

A mirror's cracked, but so am I,
Reflecting bits of crazy joy,
I grin at my own silly face,
And wonder why I'm not a toy.

The fridge hums loud with little thoughts,
Of dinners missed and snacks untold,
Among the leftovers of my dreams,
Is a chicken that's far too bold.

I sip my tea, it steams with doubt,
And contemplate my sock's existence,
Do they mate or simply just roam?
It's such a sock and yarn persistence.

My brain's a circus on a roll,
With clowns that trip and jokes to hold,
I laugh until I spill my drink,
Introspection's way too uncontrolled.

The Journey Beyond

I packed my bag with whispers of hope,
And all the snacks I could procure,
Setting out to find what lies ahead,
While asking if I've packed enough cure.

The road is paved with caution signs,
That warn of pitfalls along the way,
But I skip right past and sing a tune,
As if the world's my grand ballet.

With all the maps I cannot read,
I wander off, somewhat absurd,
As geese honk loudly, sharing tales,
Of adventures often unheard.

Each wrong turn becomes a laugh,
As I discover paths so wide,
It's a dance of chaos, fun, and cheer,
The journey's more fun than the ride.

Embracing Impermanence

A cupcake sits, adorned in sprinkles,
But watch its fate as time moves fast,
It's here for joy, then gone for sure,
In a blink, it's memories cast.

The cat ponders life from heights unknown,
With a wisdom only it can decree,
That chasing tails is a perfect quest,
But should it last eternally?

Each tick of time is a silly joke,
As birthday candles melt with glee,
We light them up, then blow them out,
Embracing thus our folly spree.

So here's to laughter and fleeting sights,
To moments shared, then swept away,
For in this dance of crazy spins,
We find the joy in each child's play.

Mosaic of Moments

In the morning, toast in hand,
I ponder deep, I just can't stand.
A sock misplaced, my cat's aloof,
Each moment's like a broken roof.

Coffee spills, I laugh, I sigh,
A paper plane just caught the sky.
Juggling chores and dreams anew,
Is this the dance I'm meant to do?

Friends are here with wild debates,
About the best and worst of fates.
Their laughter weaves a patchwork bright,
In chaos, warmth ignites the night.

Life's a jigsaw, missing pieces,
Some days it swells, some days it ceases.
Embrace the puzzling, join the mess,
In quirky moments, we find success.

The Paradox of Purpose

Why chase a dream that's out of reach?
When life feels like a grand coach breach.
I try to plan, I try to plot,
But end up lost in the coffee pot.

With every goal, a curveball flies,
My cat's an expert at disguise.
Today I strive to find my plot,
But last week's plans just hit the spot!

I build a tower made of cheese,
Hoping its height will surely please.
But as it wobbles, I can't ignore,
The giggles from the friend next door.

In search of meaning, we often roam,
While tripping on our socks from home.
In this absurdity, we engage,
Laughing loud upon life's stage.

Sunlight through the Storm

A storm rolls in, the sky's a mess,
I dance around in my Sunday dress.
Raindrops fall on my ice cream cone,
As if nature just called my phone.

But sunlight breaks, the world's aglow,
With puddles that reflect the show.
I skip and jump, a joyous spree,
Wondering how it came to be.

Umbrellas flip, they flip and flop,
Yet laughter's louder than the drop.
In every shower, there's a grin,
Finding joy where it begins.

So let it rain, let thunder boom,
I'll dance away, in this room.
Through storms we find the brightest hue,
A rainbow smile, bold and true.

Beneath the Weight of Stars

Under stars, I ponder schemes,
While chugging on my cup of dreams.
Gravity's here, but so is chance,
Encouraging a nightly dance.

The universe whispers, 'Take a peek,'
At all the things that seem so bleak.
A comet swoops, it sings a tune,
Amidst the chaos, we find the moon.

I trip on thoughts, but do I mind?
My scattered ideas are hard to find.
Like socks in dryer, lost in space,
Each thought a star, a quirky place.

So here's to stargazing in our weird way,
Embracing questions that twist and sway.
In cosmic jest, we laugh, we roam,
Finding comfort in the unknown.

Embracing the Unknown

In moments dark, we dance and prance,
With twirls and spins, we dare to chance.
A sock is lost, a shoe won't fit,
The coffee spills—oh, what a hit!

We laugh at fate, it can't be tamed,
With every plot twist, we're unashamed.
Chasing shadows, we play our game,
As fortune winks, we stake our claim.

Let's toast to chaos, the untamed ride,
With giggles shared and fears aside.
For in the mess, our joy resides,
And all we need is a friend beside.

So here's to chance, a wild embrace,
With life's quirks lending us their grace.
In this circus, we find our throne,
Together, navigating the great unknown.

The Weight of Words

A whisper here can change the scene,
Like puns that tease the in-between.
A jest, a jibe, can spark a fight,
Or tickle ribs till late at night.

Each letter carries baggage, oh,
Like a suitcase stuffed with odds and flow.
A compliment can lift you high,
While critique ties you down to sigh.

So choose your phrases, like fine wine,
Opt for the sweet, let the sour shine.
In laughter's realm, just take a leap,
The words we wield, our secrets keep.

For in the banter, we find our truth,
Crafted like stories from our youth.
Make merry with your phrase parade,
And let the blush of laughter invade.

Ghosts of Yesterday

Old photos laugh from dusty frames,
With cheesy smiles and silly games.
Each moment frozen, stuck in time,
Reminds us all, life's not a crime.

They haunt us still, those years gone by,
With fashion faux pas, oh my, oh my!
Yet in those ghosts, we find our muse,
A chuckle blooms in what we choose.

Stuck in high school like a broken clock,
Trade "who wore it best?" for laughter's stock.
As memories dance like waltzing flames,
We toast to pasts, with all their claims.

So let them linger, these playful shades,
In every dance, our joy cascades.
With echoes that share a wink and grin,
Those ghosts remind us where we've been.

Flickers of Hope

In candlelight, we seek the spark,
With every joke, we light the dark.
A silly slip can change the flow,
And laughter's warmth begins to glow.

When storms arise, we stand in line,
With umbrellas turned to caps divine.
For every drizzle brings a cheer,
We splash in puddles, drawing near.

Those tiny flames, they dance and tease,
With each warm laugh, we catch the breeze.
A wink, a nod, like fireflies,
Igniting joy beneath gray skies.

So here's to hope in every jest,
In tangled knots, we find our zest.
With every giggle, we chase the light,
Unraveling joy, from day to night.

The Weight of Unsaid Words

In the silence, thoughts collide,
Heavy whispers rather hide.
Socks mismatched, yet they smile,
Words untold travel a mile.

Coffee spills on Monday's grind,
Lost the plot, but hey, I'm fine.
Tell a joke, they laugh out loud,
What's the point? I'm feeling proud.

A cat strolls by, steals my show,
Unspoken truths, oh where'd they go?
Yet in the chaos, laughter brews,
Finding comfort in the blues.

So here's a toast to what we miss,
The funny games of silent bliss.
Raise your glass, let's make a fuss,
In this tangled web, it's just us.

Searching in a Sea of Stars

Sailing 'cross the cosmic streams,
With a map drawn in silly dreams.
Stars fall down like clumsy fools,
Wishing wells and hippie schools.

Galaxies are not so bright,
When you're lost on a Tuesday night.
Pigs can fly, I question that,
Yet here I sit, lost with a cat.

Time's a jester, throwing pies,
In the face of wise old guys.
Grab a star, make a wish,
Oh wait, that's just a flying fish.

In the end, what have we found?
Just a mirage spinning 'round.
So grab a snack, enjoy the glee,
While we dance with destiny.

Chasing Shadows of Forgotten Days

In the dusk, shadows tease and play,
Whispers of what went astray.
Chasing echoes, what a jest,
Faded memories wear a vest.

Yesterday called, I didn't reply,
Had a date with a chicken pie.
Time's a prankster, twists and bends,
But my laughter never ends.

Footprints linger on the floor,
Like a sock that begs for more.
Finding joy amidst the mess,
Who knew chaos could impress?

So here's to shadows and their prance,
Waltzing with a happy chance.
Take a bow, and let us sing,
For all the chaos laughter brings.

The Color of Ambivalence

Dancing in shades of gray and blue,
Is it happy? Is it true?
Life's a painting, brush off stray,
In confusion, we find our sway.

It's a circus, colors clash,
With a compliment and a bash.
Caught between the wrong and right,
I'll wear stripes on polka night.

Orange socks with plaid ensemble,
Do we fit? I can't quite ramble.
Waving flags of doubt and cheer,
While reasoning just disappears.

So here we dance, a lovely mess,
In ambivalence, we find our zest.
Paint us with all shades unknown,
In humor, we've truly grown.

Sifting Through Sand

In the desert we play, throwing grains,
Hiding truths in laughter, dodging pains.
The sun's a jokester, burning our skin,
While we ponder where to begin.

A mirage appears, oh what a tease,
Promises of wisdom, a breeze through the trees.
With each step forward, the ground shifts high,
Ticklish thoughts float as clouds drift by.

We sift and we stir, looking for gold,
But find quirky tales that never get old.
In a sandbox of choices, we trip and fall,
Collecting our wisdom with nothing at all.

So let's laugh at the feasts served on sand,
Embracing confusion, make confusion our brand.
For amidst all the chaos, joy takes its stand,
In the glorious mess of this whimsical land.

The Pulse of the Present

Tick-tock, tick-tock, the clock's spinning round,
With moments that leap, flip, twist, and astound.
Inside our own heads, chaos unwinds,
Pulses of thought like popcorn that binds.

The now is a creature both curious and sly,
Winking at us as we dance on the fly.
But wait, what's this feeling? Is it fear or delight?
Oh, it's just my dinner trying to take flight.

Each second's a joke, a playful little jest,
While we chase our own tails with hope for the best.
We laugh with the universe, crazy and bold,
In the heartbeat of chaos, countless stories unfold.

So here in the moment, let's bend and let sway,
Joke with the present, make light of the fray.
For amidst all the madness, let laughter resolve,
In the dance of absurdity, we're destined to evolve.

Bridges of Tomorrow

Building bridges of hope with spaghetti strands,
While dodging the raindrops with clumsy hands.
Tomorrow looks funny, dressed up in dreams,
A puppet show ready, bursting at the seams.

We draw plans with crayons, all colors and shapes,
As the future giggles, dressed up as grapes.
With wobbly stilts, we promise to try,
To balance our hearts under a lollipop sky.

But ah, what a trip, the path isn't straight,
With cupcakes for anchors and jellybean fate.
Yet we traverse the quirks, the puns, and the cheers,
With laughter the laughter, dissolving our fears.

So, side by side, let's skip into the sun,
Crafting bridges of nonsense while we laugh and run.
For in the tangled journey, the joy intertwines,
In the playful tomorrow, where friendship aligns.

Kaleidoscope of Thoughts

Twists and turns in a wild little scroll,
Thoughts swirling together, a whimsical shoal.
With giggles and snickers, we ponder and pause,
Unraveling whispers like confetti, just because.

A laugh at the ready, a smile in dispute,
As ideas dance freely, even in loot.
We juggle the nonsense, parade the bizarre,
In a carnival of colors, we're all a memoir.

But wait, is that reason peeking around?
Dressed in a tutu, it stands on the ground.
With each spin and twist, we tumble through glee,
A kaleidoscope journey — come, join me, please!

So let's treasure the laughter, the quirky and bright,
In the chaos of dreams, we'll surely ignite.
For in this zany puzzle where thoughts lightly sway,
Humor weaves wisdom — it's all just a play.

Navigating the Grey

In a world of black and white,
I can't find my shades,
Like socks that lost their mates,
I dance with the wild parades.

The compass spins, what a twist!
Directions lost in a fog,
I followed the signs too close,
And now I jog with a dog.

Laughing at the wisdom books,
Written by folks in their thirties,
While I'm stuck in toddler giggles,
And searching for my keys and jellies.

Navigating life's odd paths,
With a map that's upside-down,
So I'll skip through the chaos,
In a party hat and gown.

Reflections in a Rainy Mirror

A puddle shows my bright green shoes,
Yet spilled coffee dims the view,
I seek the silver lining here,
But it bubbles like old stew.

Raindrops chat with my umbrella,
Negotiating terms for fun,
Each drop a witty little friend,
Saying, 'Hey, wanna run?'

My hair's a frizzed-out art display,
With a hint of drama queen,
Hoping that the sun will come,
To wash away this scene.

Splashes mean a powdery face,
A clown at a magic show,
Oh how the reflection shifts,
As I dance in the downpour flow.

Beneath the Facade of Simplicity

Behind my smile lies a riddle,
Like a cat who plays the fiddle,
Caught in the web of my own thoughts,
I laugh, but sanity's brittle.

Oh, how joy wears a silly hat,
Pretending to do the splits,
While chaos trips on the welcome mat,
Taking clumsy little hits.

Beneath a grin so very wide,
Lurks a dopey little clown,
Forever juggling life's great fears,
With a smile turned upside-down.

Shuffling cards of hopes and dreams,
While the pot is boiling dry,
I chuckle at the irony here,
As I give adulting a try.

Juggling Dreams and Reality

I toss my dream up to the stars,
But it lands in the neighbor's yard,
Barking dogs and laundry lines,
Oh, juggling ironies are hard!

With one hand holding childish hope,
And the other wrapped in bills,
I dance like I'm a wild goose chase,
Tripping on my own frills.

The stage is set, but I forgot,
My lines amid the crowd,
So I find my balance on the brink,
With an applause that's not too loud.

Juggling twists of fate and chance,
While wearing mismatched socks,
I'll laugh at life's absurd romance,
As I spin like a thousand clocks.

In the Company of Questions

Why is the sky so wide and blue?
Yet my socks vanish, just like my shoe?
Is cereal soup? Oh, who would know?
And why can't I find the remote, though?

If ducks can quack and still have pride,
Can I get lost on a straightened ride?
Do dreams come true like stories say?
Or do they just giggle and dash away?

Is time a friend, or just a tease?
Can I have coffee without the freeze?
If laughter is best, why do we sigh?
And why do we fear the number five?

Questions dance like flies in June,
Buzzing sweetly, a silly tune.
So raise a glass to sense and nonsense,
I'll sip my drink, with no regrets hence!

The Art of Untangling

I tried to braid my spaghetti, oh dear,
It's all a tangle, must be the beer!
If I tie my shoes while standing still,
Will gravity laugh? Is that the thrill?

Attempting to sort out all my thoughts,
Like herding cats or tying knots.
Do I scribble in shades of the bizarre?
Or just watch the world from my couch, ajar?

Twisting and turning like a bad dance move,
My brain's a maze, so hard to improve.
If I sway left, will the answers unfold?
Or is it wise to just let go, be bold?

So here I am, a friendly mess,
Accepting chaos, my only guess.
With a wink of mirth, I'll wear my crown,
For tangled threads make the best renown!

Threads of Tomorrow

Tomorrow's threads are colorful, bright,
Yet here I am, lost in the night.
If I jump ahead, will I trip or glide?
Or just find myself on a bumpy ride?

The future laughs, while I sit tight,
Sipping coffee, avoiding the fright.
If my planner's full, do I look like a pro?
Or does it just hint that I'm in the woe?

Dreaming of journeys, big and small,
Will my GPS ever hear my call?
Or will I wander with style, not haste?
Imagine the laughs! Oh, what a taste!

So let's toast to the unknown we face,
With humor and joy, it's a grand embrace.
The threads may tangle or weave a fine tale,
In this grand adventure, we shall prevail!

Between the Lines of Clarity

Between the lines, where wisdom hides,
Is it truth or just my brain that glides?
If I read too fast, will sense arise,
Or will it giggle and roll its eyes?

In search of clarity, I sip my tea,
Wondering if it's just me being me.
If I ponder too long, will I miss the fun?
Or just find clarity on the run?

Like finding Waldo in every crowd,
Or winning the lottery—feel so proud!
Can I decode the secret glow?
Or should I just dance like no one knows?

So here's to the journey, uncharted still,
With humor and curiosity, a mighty thrill.
May we laugh at the puzzles, the absurd and clear,
And celebrate clarity, with joy and cheer!

When Stars Align and Collide

When stars align, chaos brews,
Planets dance in mismatched shoes.
Jupiter's lost his sense of style,
While Saturn grins in cosmic guile.

Eclipses laugh, hiding from sight,
Comets prance in sheer delight.
Cosmic jester with twinkling eye,
As meteors chuckle in the sky.

Galaxies clash with flair and sass,
While black holes gulp down hope in mass.
Starry knights joust in a spin,
'Tis all a game, let the fun begin!

So here's to chaos, an astral spree,
In this universe, wild and free.
Laugh with the stars, let worries fade,
For in this mess, joy is made.

The Puzzle with Missing Pieces

A jigsaw of life on the dining table,
With pieces that fit as well as they're able.
One shaped like pizza, another like toast,
And yet, it's this puzzling we love the most.

The edges are lost, and corners don't chat,
A cat snuck off with the piece of the hat.
Colors are wrong, and I've lost the plot,
Yet laughter arises from this jumbled spot.

Mom says it's fun, a family affair,
While Dad grumbles loud from his armchair.
Finding the pieces, we stumble and dive,
Creating a mess that somehow feels alive.

So here's to the puzzle, the chaos we claim,
In each missing piece, there's laughter and game.
For every odd shape holds stories untold,
In this quirky creation, our hearts unfold.

Between Joy and Sorrow's Edge

Between joy's leap and sorrow's sigh,
A tightrope walker with a pie in the sky.
Smiles tumble down like a clumsy clown,
While frowns on pillows wear a sleepy crown.

The sun may shine, yet clouds might scoff,
As rainbows giggle in the on-and-off.
Ecstatic chuckles dance past frowns,
In this circus of feelings, we wear our crowns.

Bananas peel with laughter's embrace,
Finding joy in each awkward place.
As comedy and tragedy intertwine,
In this blend of chaos, we craft our design.

So let's juggle the laughs and the tears,
For each silly moment's worth it, my dears.
Swaying on edges, we dare to engage,
Between joy and sorrow, we write our page.

The Paradox of Tomorrow

Tomorrow's promise is a jolly old fool,
While today's antics break every rule.
Plans are made with glitter and glue,
Yet chaos creeps in, as it often will do.

Calendars laugh, as time goes astray,
While old clocks tick-tock in a wobbly way.
Future's a tale that twists and spins,
With hope in our pockets, the laughter begins.

Dreams collide in a vapor of haste,
As reality's cake has too much paste.
Balloons float high, then promptly deflate,
Yet joyfully pouting, we still celebrate.

So raise your glass to the whims of the hour,
For the paradox blooms with chaotic power.
In tomorrow's mischief, we revel and play,
As the sun sets on today's cabaret.

The Dance of Shadows

In the twilight, shadows sway,
Chasing giggles, led astray.
They twist and turn, a playful spree,
While the sun laughs, 'Come dance with me!'

A wobbly waltz, a silly jig,
Each step a mystery, oh so big!
They trip and tumble, a comical sight,
As moonlight chuckles, 'Hold on tight!'

Whispers of joy drift through the air,
Barefoot dancers, without a care.
The night unfolds with quirky flair,
In this grand show, we're all laid bare.

So spin and sway, forget the rules,
Embrace the chaos, join the fools.
For in this dance, we find the key,
To laugh away life's mystery.

Whispers of the Unfathomable

Upon a breeze, thoughts take flight,
Words exchange, day turns to night.
Silly secrets, secrets so rich,
Laughter echoing, oh, what a hitch!

In the corners of the mind, we play,
Mixing whispers in a light-hearted fray.
Confusion reigns, but what does it matter?
A riddle wrapped in a giggle-chatter.

What's that sound? A thought gone rogue,
Riding trains with a comical brogue.
Lost in the maze of our own delight,
We trip on questions that take flight.

So let us ponder and jest, my friend,
For in this nonsense, joys never end.
The unfathomable's just a grand charade,
Where laughter reigns, and worries fade.

Fleeting Moments

A wink, a nod, a glance that lingers,
Silly stories told by finger singers.
Moments buzz like bees on the run,
Each one a puzzle, but oh, so fun!

Tomorrow's a trickster, today's a tease,
Whispering secrets on the gentle breeze.
Savor the giggles, let worries float,
In these fleeting moments, we all emote.

Tickle a thought, give a giggle chase,
Seeing life in a silly place.
What's this, a riddle wrapped in a tune?
Dancing through the chaos, oh, the maroon!

Each breath a spark, a whimsy flare,
Caught in the nets of time's great snare.
So stitch these moments, make them bright,
With laughter woven in the light.

Endless Questions

What comes first, the egg or the joke?
Tangled thoughts, like yarn, provoke.
Why do socks vanish in the wash?
Questions bubble, dissolve, and nosh.

We ponder worlds where cats wear hats,
And find the meaning in playful spats.
Such riddle quests turn serious ground,
Yet laughter blooms where answers are drowned.

Why is it that ice cream melts so fast?
As sweet as wonder, but shadows are cast.
Giggles chase answers, like kittens in flight,
While the universe winks, just out of sight.

So toss those queries in the air,
Sprinkle joy—there's more to share.
For in this game of ask and grin,
The end of questions means the fun's about to begin!

Beneath the Surface of Ordinary

Underneath the calm, bubbles rise,
A world of wonder behind sleepy eyes.
The mundane vibrates with secrets untold,
Where joy lurks around every fold.

Dishes pile high, but who really cares?
A kingdom of chaos, with whimsical flares.
Mismatched socks may win the grand prize,
In this circus where logic defies.

A coffee spill? A splash of grace!
In the art of mishaps, we find our place.
Laughter bubbles up from ordinary scenes,
With each little hiccup, adventure redeems.

So peek beneath the laughter, my friend,
In the ordinary, find the blend.
Where every sparkle's a treasure unfold,
Making the dull a little more bold.

Secrets of the Unseen Path

We wander in circles, feet in a mess,
Chasing our tails, what a funny stress.
The trees whisper secrets, their leaves take a bow,
"These branches mean something, just don't ask us how!"

With maps full of squiggles and X's on ground,
We dig up the laughter, it's silly and sound.
Each path that we take seems to lead to a joke,
"Oops, not the treasure! Just another old cloak!"

The stars wink above us, a cosmic charade,
Each twinkle a riddle we've all mislaid.
"To find what you seek, watch your feet, not your head!"
A sign made of stardust, quite cleverly said.

So here's to the journey, with giggles and glee,
With wrong turns and hiccups, oh how can that be?
Let's toast to confusion, our baffling dance,
For secrets unfold in a fit of sheer chance!

The Intricacies of a Single Breath

Inhale, exhale, what a strange little game,
A hiccup, a snort, it's all just the same.
One breath in the morning could lead to a yawn,
While others erupt with a sneeze at the dawn.

Each puff full of wonders, like bubbles in air,
What's floating around? Is that Zorro? A bear?
We chuckle and wheeze with each frolicsome puff,
As wisdom eludes us, we just huff and bluff.

The rhythm of life in this wheezy song,
Is beautifully awkward, but who's keeping strong?
With gasps and deep breaths, we flutter with cheer,
"Don't ask for a meaning, just relish the air!"

So let's breathe together and giggle some more,
Our lungs are a theater, oh what a score!
In every sweet gasp is a mystery cast,
As we burp our way through, let's raise a glass fast!

In Search of Elusive Truths

With magnifying glasses and conspiracy hats,
We hunt for the answers like curious cats.
Each truth that we find has a riddle attached,
And lo and behold, it's a puzzle unmatched!

Captured in whispers and flutters of fate,
The truth wears a mustache, isn't that great?
We chase after shadows, they giggle and flee,
It's a comedy sketch, oh it's scoffingly free!

A fortune cookie burps out some wise little line,
But when we break open, it's just about wine.
With every new fact that we think we've unspooled,
The universe snickers, we're just being fooled!

So here's to the seekers, the goofy and brave,
For truth's just a riddle, with laughter to save.
Round up your puzzles, your giggles, your kits,
For truths are just jokes that the cosmos admits!

Fragments of a Fractured Soul

Once a puzzle, now bits scattered wide,
Each shard holds a story, no place left to hide.
With pieces that sparkle, some jagged and rough,
This soul's a collector of laughably tough!

A heart's like a ham, a punchline it seems,
It squeaks when it squeezes, oh, filled with wild dreams.
A jester in the mirrors, reflectively cracked,
"Is this who we are? Or just humor attacked?"

The fragments they giggle, so bright, so absurd,
With quirks and odd murmurs, it's all gotten blurred.
Embracing the chaos, we tiptoe and prance,
"Let's waltz with our quirks, in this fractured romance!"

For though we are scattered, it's funny, I'd say,
These pieces together form a grand cabaret.
So toast to the fractures, and laugh with the whole,
For each little segment is part of the soul!

The Tapestry of Existence

In the loom of the day, I weave and I spin,
Mixing laughter with chaos, a dance to begin.
With tangled up threads and quirks in the weave,
I chuckle at patterns I hardly believe.

The colors are bright, yet the knots are absurd,
Knitting confusion, it seems quite preferred.
Each strand tells a joke, some serious too,
Embroidered with wisdom and glitter from glue.

I ponder the why while I trip on a stitch,
Waltzing through questions, not rich but still rich.
In this tapestry, life throws shades every day,
I giggle at choices and fa-la-la away.

So here I shall sit, with my needle and thread,
Laughing at thoughts that dance in my head.
The tapestry unfolds, a spectacular show,
With mishaps and hopes that ebb and then flow.

Threads of Uncertainty

In the closet of thoughts, I find quite a mess,
With threads of unsure that I must confess.
I tug on a line, it frays and it twirls,
Unraveling patterns like dizzying swirls.

A sock here, a button, and a plan gone awry,
Yet laughter erupts with a whimsical sigh.
For every loose end is a reason to grin,
In the fabric of doubts, the fun can begin.

The weaver's a joker, with hands spinning fate,
Entwining the silly with serious weight.
I trip on my thoughts, but I smile with glee,
For even mishaps seem perfect to me.

Each thread tells a story, a twist in the tale,
Of silver linings wrapped up in a veil.
So let loose those threads that tickle the mind,
In uncertainty's dance, the joy is entwined.

Labyrinths of the Heart

In the maze of emotions, I wander and roam,
With a map that's upside down, I'm searching for home.
A turn here, a twist, and a bump on the way,
Yet chuckling at each misstep wants to play.

I see signs that point to some sentimental bliss,
But all I uncover is a cheeky kiss.
With pathways of hope that lead back to the start,
I stumble on truths in this maze of my heart.

The walls are quite narrow, but laughter is free,
Each corner I peek brings out more of me.
For what's a good labyrinth without a good jest?
Fumbling with feelings, I'm truly quite blessed.

So here I will linger, with quirks and some sighs,
In the labyrinth's grip, I discover my highs.
With funny reflections and riddles unspun,
I embrace the absurd, for we're never outdone.

Echoes in an Empty Room

In the quietest corners of space and of time,
The echoes ring out, some silly, some rhyme.
I giggle with shadows, they dance on their own,
Making friends with the whispers, I'm never alone.

In the emptiness, jokes bounce off the walls,
With punchlines that follow, like bouncing beach balls.
Each giggle of silence brings joy to the air,
As I waltz in the echoes without a care.

The room may feel vacant, yet full of good cheer,
With giggles and guffaws that only I hear.
I chatter with nothing and chat for a while,
With humor that travels, I'm greeted with style.

So here I will linger, let echoes drum loud,
In the theater of solitude, I laugh with the crowd.
For what's in an echo but joy that's set free?
In the stillness, I find my own company.

Reflections in a Broken Mirror

In a funhouse, I stare at my grin,
Who is that? I can't let them in.
My hair's a bird's nest, eyes askew,
I laugh so hard, the glass cracks too.

Life throws pies, with whipped cream cheer,
Each slice a mystery, oh dear, oh dear!
The clown's behind me, wig's askew,
He shrugs and grins, what's one more view?

In a world where quirks dance like fire,
The mundane's a jester, never to tire.
I play the fool, gladly and loud,
In the circus of dreams, I'm proud and unbowed.

So here's to the cracks that let us see,
That the best reflections are a little cheeky.
With laughter as glue, we piece the plot,
And find the meaning in the funny and hot.

A Symphony of Doubt

A kazoo plays softly in my head,
Is this a tune or a long string of dread?
The orchestra's tuning, but wait, oh dear,
My thoughts respond with a honk and a sneer.

The conductor's lost, waving his baton,
Is that a note or a lawn needing dawn?
Each question echoes, a baffling beat,
While I dance in circles, shuffling my feet.

I scribble my notes on a crumpled page,
Witty remarks from a circus age.
The melody's quirky, the rhythm's absurd,
Each note a riddle, each silence unheard.

Yet amidst this chaotic fiddle-faddle,
There's humor in doubt, let's jump in the saddle.
With each wobbly step, we create our song,
In this symphony sweet, where we all belong.

Chasing Fleeting Horizons

I chase a sunset on a pogo stick,
Hopping with glee, this should do the trick!
But the horizon giggles, just out of reach,
Teases me gently like a sly speech.

I trade my worries for some dancing feet,
Sprinting toward sunsets, oh, what a feat!
But shadows play hide-and-seek with my dreams,
While laughter erupts from time's crazy schemes.

The stars are my map, the moon is my guide,
Yet every lost moment is a jolly ride.
With laughter my compass, I twirl and sway,
In pursuit of the hues that lead me astray.

So here's to the chase, the wink of the sky,
To missed connections that make us fly.
In ducking and dodging, we learn and grow,
As horizons invite us to steal the show.

The Jigsaw of Journeys

In a box labeled 'journeys,' I pull out a piece,
It doesn't quite fit, but what a release!
With colors that clash and patterns askew,
I chuckle and giggle, what next will I do?

Each twist of fate's like a puzzle gone mad,
Some pieces are joyful, some simply sad.
But in this grand game, I've come to find,
That laughter's the glue of the jigsaw kind.

To fit in the corners, I've taken some jabs,
While lost little edges cling like scrappy drabs.
Each piece tells a story, some silly, some sweet,
In the mix of our mishaps, we dance on our feet.

So let's raise a toast to this colorful mess,
For without the odd shapes, we'd truly regress.
In the jigsaw of joy, let each piece reside,
Where laughter retains what time cannot hide.

www.ingramcontent.com/pod-product-compliance
Lightning Source LLC
Chambersburg PA
CBHW072217070526
44585CB00015B/1378